I0192070

Dark Man Blues

Copyright © 2017 by Samuel Benjamin
All rights reserved under International and Pan-American
Copyright Conventions. Published in the United States by
Innate Divinity,
All of the poems in this collection, excluding the titles
are Copyright © by Samuel Benjamin and are reprinted by
permission of Innate Divinity and Dark Man Blues The Series. No part of this
publication may be reproduced or transmitted in any form or by any means
– electronic, mechanical, photocopying, recording, or otherwise – without
the written permission of the publisher.
ISBN-13: 978-0999601815 (Innate Divinity)
ISBN-10: 0999601814

Dark Man Blues: if it were me

Samuel Rain Benjamin

INNATE DIVINITY

San Bernardino/Houston

In Loving Memory of Jason Jijja Scott

Brother 2 Brother

12/16/73 - 01/15/17

The Pages

Opening pages

Camouflage

Can u see it?
disguising itself
America's feelings
in living color
black white
liars cover up
exposed
most of them
say it isn't so
I beg to differ
if you
stand with them
democrat's, republican's
whichever wing
birds
one in the same
fact check me if you want
discover the truth
faced
with a lie they can't cover up
see
the chameleons

Back 2 The Future

One Hundred and Fifty years set back
1865 you can't even cash that
everything that use 2 be
do u remember that
they may even do a movie
about that
the day America got checked
this time
we fight back . . .
no more waiting
they got plans, so do we
voting for democracy
it's a false sense
dreaming
damn that
this is going 2 b payback
my future intent
standing true
these are my thoughts
it's 3am and you
have pushed the right button

Analysis

we're like the sun

always giving

moon child rising

from this beginning

we contemplate

centuries

leaving memories

we be world

monuments

mapped from stars

life signing

mankind's destiny

they're playing us 2 close

without unity

this will end

see them

madmen

thinking

they can change

the game

Loving U

I'm going 2, love u
with all of my senses
not just the five they mention
my 360
coming in dimensions
encompassing
this loves reality
you the world and me
my . . . complicated passion
leaving traces
of existence
having one and one become three
sharing the pleasures
of passion
u surrender with me
living dreams
painting images
of just how beautiful
love should be
knowing . . . u have given
this gift of life
2 me

Dark Man Blues

Seeing the world through my eyes
being me
mind open, playing out
how society has pictured me
from ruling 2 slavery
finding myself locked in
making my own
history
true perspective
discarding the bullshit laid out
over centuries
living me
living the skin I'm in
knowing
I am a King
controlling my own destiny
protecting
my life, my
family
I've got the Dark Man Blues

Riding High

I am a story needing to be told
being every word I say
no stop signs
finding vision
knowing it, too
checking those who confront me
being inspired
by the truth
every day, living my destiny
naming names
Malcolm . . .
King . . .
and Me
owning it, speaking it
living it
no selfishness
seeing it's bigger than myself
calling people out
saying it
I'm Black and I'm proud

The Lines

Finding myself . . . read me

word playing

in the World Stage Press

my intentions

laid out

my mission: feeding your imagination

all points

uplifting

opening doors

sometimes, sharing

all forms of

expressions

touching young minds

marked for greatness

melanin driven

making dreams

while

goal-mapping

these lines

Mind Gazing

Knowing me, knowing u

scripting

my affection

loving myself

just the way I want u

on the real

not just saying

living it

got me

mind-gazing your

dreams

reading the pages

becoming

the whispers

you surrender too

having u

imagining it

seeding

the possibilities and

loving it

Defining Me

Sixty years of conditions
going through life's
attrition
defining the moments
defining me
the reflection man made
landmines to a grave
it's a trap
born free, now realizing
it was never meant
to be
the cover up
my mind
open
internet truth exposing
written lies
picture this
the stories old ones told
realness
knowing his story
ain't mine
my passport 2 freedom

Think About It

Today like yesterday
looking back on the way things used to be
like when they had slavery
picture yourself
in that
I'll wait
here's the reality:
almost 400 years of the same story
it's a got-u-moment
played out live
on TV
forget the written history
it was only written
for fools
tell a lie over and over
they will believe
remember when we couldn't read
and now we're not
reading at all
dumb them down
and then
they can't rise

The Game

Moments of an imagination

my own

if it were me . . . check mate

not being diminished

by the game

being a checker forgetting I'm a King

can u see it?

u think you made it

take away his money, where would he be?

just an old line on repeat

can u say Bill Cosby?

serving him

not serving yourself

get big

get checked

reminding others they could be next

if u don't walk

the line

game time . . . thinking you're on top

to only see

they have conditioned

your mind

Once a Slave

Free . . . at no time in this life have I been
a made-up reality
trapped on a replay
same channel
same display
disguised as "you're free now"
in a constitution
not written for me
another contract
on slavery
here's looking at you
1865
him fighting him to free me
fact check the reality
on that shit
truths coming
here's the illusion:
open carry, shot dead
live on TV
not wanting me to forget
he'll
take my life

The Symbol

I have pledged my allegiance

spoken its name

although it has no soul

we are taught to surrender

this symbol

of our freedom

and yet we

have not seen it

it speaks of liberty, I seek its justice

I may never live it

be damned if I do . . .

we have even fought

for it

its truths

voiceless

words from a past

not representing us

knowledge is a vessel

being

wasted

on a symbol . . .

When I Can Never Say No

Love called . . . said she missed me
had me thinking
I do too
waking me out of a dream
my wanting her
would echo me . . . seeing she's my daily
like the sun chasing
love's melody
I could never say no
to the mystery
back to the conversation
love called . . . said she needed some attention
said my time would be
all the things . . .
she feels
love, had a mission
she wanted
my dreams
had my emotions
asking "have you
always felt this way?"
love answered

My Command Performance

It was time to go live

to share my emotions deep

I could feel temptation

. . . falling

into every word

her eyes like

whispers

had me adlibbing

"girl, you're fine!"

caressing her like

seconds do time

I could sense her

seeping

thinking she could be my next line

loving me as if

I were her dreams

had me picturing a goldmine

being my true love

like the words

in this

rhyme

I could go on, but . . . it seems I'm out of time

Man's Last Chance

If I didn't know better
the earth . . . is telling me
calling for harmony
like nature   meant us to be
like a river flows to the sea
like honey
can only come from bees
just an analogy
mankind so emotional
warring each other
over man made religion race creed
even skin color
damn what are we doing to each other
got me thinking
obsession
this may be man's last chance
to bring anew
can someone tell me please
who's going to save
the children

13

It was a moment called freedom

another piece of paper

wordplaying

before the ink was dry

plans were made to keep slaves

marching them places

call it . . . unmarked graves

Mississippi burning, Oklahoma too

most southern states

hiding the truth

they be the government

writing books on how to keep the negro a slave

have you read it?

calling it segregation

planting that seed

time goes by

just give them a little more

maybe integration

call it civil rights; we can kill them differently

no one will know, you see

they write the history

Never

I've taken a look back
found the truth
it was all a lie . . . being taught
my history, that is
thinking they could write us out
waiting for time
to erase a past they wanted
us to forget
always making up something new until then
call it Jim Crow
after slavery, a textbook on control
keeping its mission
"never
let them grow;
"never
let them know
who
they truly are;
using our own words against us,
by any means necessary"
think about it
they have

Anticipation

She needed a distraction
she needed some more . . . complicated passions
so, I began to
caress her
imagination
one thought at a time
the words
seemed to take her
I'm thinking . . . anticipation
my temptation
whispering
"how do you love me . . . after
you make love 2 me?"
as my emotions
danced in her mind
I could sense
something beautiful
inside of her
those moments
would be my dreams
after all she was now living
the reality

The Rest of My Life

I love your hair and
the way you
wear it
even if its short, I'll still
run my fingers
through it
to look into your eyes
I would gaze with
delight
your lips, I would kiss until
I hit that spot
I want to be in every word
you speak
I want to be your living
Fantasy. as I
explore every hill and valley
peaks too
I won't stop until I discover
every part of you, that
inside view
seeing it's your imagination
I'm in to

I'll Be Reading U

Share with me
the moments of your desire
one page
at a time
let's begin
with the contents
of your mind
those moments you hide
behind the smile
before
I give in
this is where
my journey
will begin
souls connecting
through
your eyes
to capture the unspoken dreams
making you
come alive one word
at a time
so . . . I'll be reading u

Become the words I
can't write down
feel the moments of
my imagination
as my heart calls for
love's ultimatum
2007

Say you love me and I
will forever be
the next breath you take
2008

If I were making love
you would be
the only recipe I need
2010

as I uncomplicate your thoughts
know this
I am the protector
of your heart
2014

My Deepest Ocean

The me that's n 2 u
daring temptation just 2 say
I want 2
chasing the realities
of a dream
picturing my deepest
come true
having it be
sharing your life
with me
living my intentions
drowning
in your emotions, while
speaking
my affections
seeing u as my ocean
taking chances
taking a Queen
being your King
loving u just the way
you're dreaming
those Dark Man Blues

Holocaust 1619-201?

There's a block in history
it was called slavery
you see, it never ended. when you are
still living in it
they say you are free
check that
it's called "the system"
from plantation to ghetto living
all the names in
between
they even let you read it
no truth in it
made America great
poverty living
fight the wars
still, you have no dignity
you're just that
formality
he wishes he could change
in the game
he's playing
you in Holocaust

No Reply

Face the Nation
Status
Redefining who I am
my legal standing
still
second class
wait
I thought I had rights
I've come to this
understanding
knowing America never keeps its word
no justice
not even a trail
shot dead
why?
for the color of my skin
this has to end
with or without you
here's my reply
the only virus upon this land
must be purged

The Illusion

I'm calling it
wrong place, wrong time
seems to be America's bad rhyme
history playing itself out
again
the above statement
say's it all
another soul taken
"I feared for my life" that same old song
after they shoot another one
Dead
now here's the illusion
he looks like a
bad dude
wait
without a gun
you've been categorized
one of them . . . sun
can't be undone
think about it . . . if you were a white one
can you say
"beanbag?"

Death By Color

Some will say "not
in America"
the land of freedom
even though they wrote it down
it has never come to be
we have always known the truth
she's hiding
behind a lie
remember I said Civil Rights
gave them the right to kill you differently
once a slave, always to be
like the past
a good one is a dead one
my last stand
no more asking why
so many tears
drowning
in fear
this old saying
"judged and not carried"
which one will
you be?

A Different Me

I come anew
unlike something or somebody else
I'm the one
distinct and diverse
one day, someone will write about me
telling the world
he made love beautiful again
seeing
with an open
mind
translation
loving one another
never judging
giving thought to why
I share my heart
always thinking it could be me
being
the someone
on the outside looking in
asking
the question . . .
why me?

Self, Conversation

It was a moment to have this talk
with myself
I needed to think out loud
speaking truth
not everyone will
agree
we all think differently
this world
on the verge of coming
to an end
as we know it
how we see each other
with eyes open and yet, our minds
are closed
yes, I needed this moment to
think out loud
wondering if anyone
thinks like me
the way we're playing it
someone else
will write our history
the day Black stops being said

Where I'm Coming From

I have the emotions of a love poem

some say its my charm

word playing

with imagination

sometimes, complicated

my passion

like a river

having it

makes me

complete

some say

you're just a freak

it's my

surrender, whispering

the moments

of my hunger

to feel the essence of my soul

drowning

n 2 u

deep

now that's

where I'm coming from

Exposed

It would b come the rhythm
of my life
loving u
like a dream
the music of my heart
playing your emotions, as if u were
a love poem at the tip
of my tongue
I wanted to be that kiss
tasting the moments
I would miss.
these echoes
would drown me
n every moment of u
my heart fluttered
from the anticipation
2 b the whispers
answering
your every question
exposing my
deepest
desire

Captured

I imagine romancing
my day away
daydreaming thoughts of how
beautiful u are
imagining
seeing u
as my morning smile
wanting
like spring
embracing your tenderness
with a kiss
taking your next breath as
my own
so sensuous
the warmth of your
emotions flowing
with every echo
of my name
as the night
consumes me

say my name

The Biggest Part of Me

I have never loved this deep

after the moments of

a love poem

until I had you

surrendering

n 2 my arms

whispering

I am here for u

my emotions tempted

by your charm

knowing all the while

I could not resist

becoming every moment

I had dreamed

loving you into ecstasy

in words

I could never say

to have your emotions telling me

how much

my wanting you would

come 2

just being me

Living U

I am driven by these emotions
living
every word I say
with
intentions
love being my hunger
I
am an emotional
creature
embracing the surrender
I call for
passion makes me
having love
take me
like thunder
you be my storm
the moment you whisper
please
I'll be the
echo
in your dreams

N U

My everyday
being the emotions
I hunger
2 have truly found
my desire
given who I am
my   only demand
I want u
like that saying
head 2 toe
my surrender will tell u
without words
the glow inside of me
my personality
u.n.i.t.y
together, that forever
whispering it
when "love me, please"
is everything and
I've got u
daydreaming
my name

Writing N 2 Her

I'm writing this poem like a love song
loving the mystery
her eyes
are telling me
being that FM all the time
tune 2 her frequency
verbalizing my emotions
writing n 2 her
affections
making them passionately
my own
like the hook in a love song
even pleasuring
some R&B
going by the stars in her eyes
seeing she's the
love poem
I want 2 take home
I could only say
u turn me on
so, let's continue to write this poem
like a love song

Love and the Condition

She wanted my attention
it was every moment I spoke about
thinking she could turn
the passion out
passionately
I became that
surrender
my thoughts
even if it was a sin
I knew we would be friends
Then, she whispered, "you
need to give in"
had me wanting, like the next phase
with intentions
sharing all the moments
I dreamed her into
submission
thinking, "how many kisses?"
roleplaying, like
"you're going to miss me.
the next time, you'll want this
without conditions"

Loving U . . . A Blind Mans Story

Yes, it's true: I'm going 2 love you
with all my senses
that's right
not just the five
they mention
here's my 360- loving u in dimensions
while I inhale
the essence that makes you
just to feel
how the air moves
around you
as I
capture
the melodies of
your heartbeat
giving into the vibrations
surrounding me
this was the moment
I began to
discover your harmony
like a blind man
would do. now turn the page as I whisper

into you

tasting

your intentions

from a kiss

confessing my surrender

to arouse

your

femininity

word-playing your

emotions, as I

encompass

your thoughts

while embracing

the aura within

your dreams

whispering, "you're my only"

at the edge

of every breath I take

as I exhale

every thought

I'm

thinking about you

More Than I Do

No one is wanting more
than I do
falling in love from a dream
having it be u
turning a now moment
into a lifetime
passion is on the menu
seeing how much
I want 2
loving like an old school love song
Marvin Gaye singing
"Let's get it on"
just like
music
saying "all I need is u"
keeping it real
being me
shaping the pages
of my
heart
those moments when u are wanting
as much as I do

Real Time Real Talk

It's a time check moment

think about it

seeing how

reality playing itself out

these days,

lies broadcast, trying to deflect

somebody slip

really?

real talk

the cats

out the bag

"shoot him"

"wait, he had a gun

well . . .

I thought

I saw one"

here's the cover up:

"he didn't

follow orders"

"I feared for my life"

real truth

He was black

Somebody's Telling You Something

Can you hear the echo?
America's undercover story
It was 2016
true colors
this is not a dream
wake up my people . . . they
out to get u
without a chance
it's called
take them out, as many as u can
Trump
got them riled up
speaking
what they truly feel
we have had enough
of this pill
they're making plans
2 kill
"make America great again" . . . that's
the theme song
code words . . . Somebody's Telling You Something
pay attention

Mad Love

Loving u like your everyday should be
the mad love I'm
thinking of
speaking it, too
feel my heart beat that sound, it's u.
in between these lines
are the moments
I want to take your mind
one thought
at a time
to say I want u
here's my
come 2:
have u ever loved like your dreams
say you want 2?
2 have these whispers calling u?
I'll make it come true
the moments your love should be
keeping that same
old feeling
singing. . .
I can make it better for u

Willie Lynch Me

This is America's legacy
Willie Lynch and his glory
the making of a slave
gave them the fear of death back then
living the same story again
twenty sixteen
his dream . . . nightmare them, they'll give in
shoot them dead on TV
let everybody see
here is your reference
the bible said so
1712 read this shit right here
control his soul
the Willie Lynch theory
alive and well
kill them black souls
this will be your end . . .
what goes around
sounds like
we've been
Lynched
again

Honey Do

She said she loved me
maybe
I was thinking
she's trying 2 game me
not wanting to
give in
I've heard that story
one 2 many
times:
"can u please get this
for me"
giving me an if
statement
seems she was looking for
a honey-do
my thoughts? you can't
complicate me.
if you want someone to be
your slave
my name
is not
him

Only Room 4 2

I was thinking. my mind took a picture
you, me
from a distance
had my attention
my thoughts, some words
I can't even mention
wanting you like
the sun
out 2 get it
my intention
the love I would surrender 2
here's the view
only room
4 2
let me snapshot that again
I know we're
just friends . . . but
I was thinking
if we could just give in
it would be
like a motion picture sequel
all over again

Determination

Loves destination
here's my definition:
wanting that
forever
giving my soul
completely
my hunger
your surrender
feel the
persuasion
like a hunter, I sense
the affection
no word-playing
my intentions
knowing my direction
is every moment
of you
translation:
out to get it like a goldmine
going in deep
like this next line
making love to your mind

Landmine

It's time to drop some bombs
just like America
taking shit out because it's in the way
tell me you see
got this new group
half of Trump supporters
call them deplorable
middle class
about to make havoc
that old prey
target practice
call it policing, I mean policy
or any kind of way
even live on TV
life in America, once again
the purge
kill as many as you can
make America
great again
wait . . .
we did that
hold up, it's time to get payback

Color Lines

I see you . . . pity you
don't see me
even though I bear your
forefather's name
caught up in
a cycle
wishing it were a dream
knowing nightmares
never come to a good end
in a dead man's game
seeking the same rights
trying with
all my might
to treat you the same
knowing the rules
you made up
didn't include
my make up
that thing
you call the American dream
has just been
fucked up

1492

An old world, discovered new
knowing
we had already been there
thinking Pangea
calling out
Africa
touching the world
can u see it?
seeds planted everywhere
pyramid dreaming
all over
here's the true story:
the sun
never setting on our journey
defining glory
1492
his new world order
2018
we're living in a false reality
making it real
maybe one day, someone
will tell the truth

My Next Book

She would read me
capturing my emotions as if
they were her own
the lines seem to come together
exposing my hunger
like questions
an open book on how I feel about passion
word-playing
the conversation
I could feel my imagination
coming together
like a puzzle
knowing she could be
the answer
I'm thinking, her pleasures
being the title of
my next book
my expressions became lyrical
the temptation
brought provocation
had me
whispering, "may I, please . . . ?"

Where I'm Coming From

I need 2 show u something
the unspoken words
between these lines
imagine the moment of my whispers
call it anticipation
my thinking
without hesitation
no indecision
in my thoughts of how
our love will be
sensing
the hunger
wanting love's danger . . . when
yes is
everything
hearing my name as it
echoes in your
dreams
waking u just 2 take u once again
knowing you're
the love poem I never
want 2 end

I long for her
like the desert rain
to quench the thirst from the fire
that burns within me
2005

Whisper my name and I
will bring the thunder
for it lives
deep inside of me
2007

when a Man loves a Woman
it should be deep with emotions
those moments she could never say no to
when you are wanting
her affection
2014

I am to be these things
your dreams alive from every temptation
your love could ever be
2014

Your Mind

I was thinking about this line
I would speak it
like I want to make love
to your mind
having these simple words
rhyme
as though it were a love song
like you're my
fantasy
whispering all the things
you do to me
saying, "you're my home,
now let's get it on"
making love, as if we were
a love poem
capturing your smile
kissing it, too
caressing you like these words
say I want 2
now, let me love you
the way
you want me 2

Making Love on a Theory

Word painting on a theory
emotion giving
seeking some complicated passions . . . that
dark man blues
my hunger
expressing how beautiful love should be
this is the way you got me
tasting the moments
I'm speaking my confession
surrendering my affections
like a love poem
penning your heart as my home
no mystery
of my wanting seeing how
it has me thinking
I could never let go
feeling the need in you
knowing that its strong in me too
note taking on a theory
just to prove
making your love beautiful . . . is all
I want 2 do

Off Paper Love

I slept with poetry last tonight

caressed her surrender

like a dream

come true

had my emotions taken

by pleasure

to hear her affectionately whispering,

"complicated passions,

you're a freak"

she would take me deep

I had intentions of never letting go

her wordplay

was my

submission

no options given

I only needed my pen

to go all in

one word, next line

scripting this dope rhyme

you see, I slept with poetry last night

because she made love

to my mind

My Loving U

From this moment, taste my imagination

it will define

my intentions

this is my mission:

loving you like a dream

being everything

I want 2 do

whispering

how I do u, while singing

my dark man blues

surrendering my day

mind-gazing it

thinking of how beautiful

u are

you're that flower

loving spring

that summer I scream

waiting for fall

knowing my winters

will be fire

these are the things you do

unconditionally

Happenstance

I found myself dreaming
something I see
everyday
painting images in my mind
this could be me
this nightmare
it's not hard to picture this
on the streets of L.A
all eyes on me and yet, no one hears
I speak it anyway:
"do you have any change?"
passed by like
like a billboard sign
too fast to read
what was truly going through my mind
just hearing the words
"spare a dime"
this is Americas sin
this life
we are living
got me one paycheck away
thinking

Open Dialogue

Love called
wanted a conversation
said 2 me
she
had intentions of
being the dream I come to
my imagination began
to dress me
love at first sight
I thought
I could feel her wanting
turning inside of me
she was
under my skin
breaking down my resistance
picturing the moment I
would give in
love said, "when you're ready,
just talk 2 me"
whispering, "I've become
your
reaction"

Mystery Loves Company

Let me fill your imagination
once more
feel my desire as I
become all the things u dream
dial me in
call it romance
call it all the moments u need 2 give in
having my hunger
satisfy u
let me in, please let me
take u from another lonely night
2 whispering ecstasy
your heart
beating
like mine
surrender 2 this event
call it
your loving me
call it the moment the world stopped
just 2 see
2 see how mystery
loves company

The Echoes

Can you hear it?
listen
calling out are
the whispers of a thousand years
speaking
the cries of ancestors
long forgotten
the past written, not my own
truths untold
seldom mention
"I am Mankind
Earth tone
in dimensions"
color line extension, that rainbow
they always mention
when they say
my name: Melanin
no longer will I live this lie
no longer will I forsake
the cries
I will end this
can u hear the echo? dark man blues

Earth Tones

I'm a dream maker
whispering:
"have u ever been
loved
like this?"
soul caressed, emotions taken
before a kiss
forever wanting, like
more
can I get 2 this?
your love and my desire . . . that
underline passion
calling me out
from this eye 2 eye
find me
drowning deep in your
affection
feel my intentions
your pleasure
being the mission
now, are u ready
for this?

Shades

I called danger out

tempted her

with charm

the anticipation

captivated me

thinking I'm the one

I was consumed by my own hunger

love was out 2 get me

she whispered,

"I know u want me"

silence became my next breath

I found myself

taken

she began 2 read my eyes

my emotions

gave me away, as if

they were

speaking my thoughts

I could feel

temptation

flowing through me

knowing . . . she's the one

Depths of a Poet

Vision taking reality making
expressing dreams
like . . . my temptation
like painting with no illusions

Loves Destination

Loves got me
on the verge of, "let me
be the one"
your world and me in it

Love Me Now

I found myself thinking . . . these emotions
my thoughts, becoming
temptation
being drunk in your imagination

What More Can I Say

Take this like u own me
turn me out
no doubt I want u
I'm about this life . . . 2 souls becoming 1

When Love Called

It happened again. that moment when
love called
she whispered
the answer
it was all I could ever be
my thoughts were
the now
thinking I could never say no
to my hunger, yet
to be awaken
by mystery
to find it was only in my dreams
had me wondering,
"could this ever be?"
longing
for her touch
to have all of these moments of passion
burning in me
coming alive . . . I paused
my destiny
became my hunger
waiting for love to call

Word Remedy

We all flow differently
some flow rhymes and call it . . . therapy
like . . . you're going 2
miss me
so . . . here's the rewind:
complicated passions making love
2 your mind
I just need a little of
your time
now . . . the mission
me going deep
we won't call it a sin
you just need 2
give in . . .
like . . . touch me
like . . . I'm going 2 touch u
the response
me coming n 2 u
wait . . . here's the recipe:
I won't stop until you're through
u see . . . I'll need u
2 come 2

6.9-Uncut

One word at a time

next line

I've got passion

on my mind

2 love her deeply

I became that surrender

giving in 2

the tender moments

she dreams

you can call it her

submission

after that first kiss

tracing

all the moments

she missed

just 2 make them

my own

you see, she's that love poem

that gave me a home

making music

on a

love song

Speak That Truth

Today, like yesterday
the world has changed
my eyes are open 2 tomorrow's future
seeing what one wants 2
making a better way
thinking, "damn,
what just happened?"
a past reborn
watching the world go by
I mean "bye"
could be a blink of the eye
like one word
(what the fuck?)
oh . . . that's three
three chances
2 get it right
we're being locked in it
no way out
fight or die; dead men don't tell no lies
the great escape
your vote
counted – even if you didn't make it

Other Poems

My N 2 U

All I want is u

taking chances, opening doors

not coming down

with the blues

me loving x y z

going n like love is crazy

about 2 give it

the whole of me

the sum of me

that beginning

that

has no end

my temptation

whispering

like,

"you're going to have

all of me

wanting more of u"

call it love

call it

my n 2 u . . . like

please

Time Stamped

The benefit of my freedom
(if I had it)
not taking this life for granted
thinking, I should be
judging others the way
they have judged me
speaking of that place, past-time
marked by history
my coming out of slavery
not even a thought
wait . . .
can u date that?
given it hasn't gotten better yet?
seeing how
black lives don't matter?
calling it
a hate group . . .?
like
we started something new
when all the hate
is coming
from u

Beautiful Blindness

She made my day

word-played me

like

temptation

the look

her eyes

that smile

had me speaking

these intentions

knowing love was out

2 get me

I found myself

blinded by

anticipation

thinking, no doubt

I was ready for this mission

her love and

my desire

adjusted views

had me

taken . . . contemplating

the next moment

Painting America

Making America great again could be America's
greatest sin
reliving its past
days gone by
coming alive, driven by what use to be
no future status
got me asking: "do you know?"
popping off words that don't mean a thing
got people wishing
on past history dreams
thinking . . .
oh, say can you see
don't under estimate my silence
over thinking you got me
having the signs paint
a false sense
of reality
not understanding what freedom
really means
seeing you have never paid
restoration for your pass crimes
committed against me

The Written Confessions Of DMB

These
spoken truths
the sharing of my imagination
that something beautiful
chasing temptation
whispering:
"I've got intentions"
writing n 2 u
loving my destination
channeling
your affections
becoming
what you dream
pleasuring everything
surrendering as if you were
my canvas
caressing the thought
of you
being taken by
the scent
of you
just to confess my love for you

Poem

I began to share
you were the conversation
me, painting off paper
like an artist
having you as my canvas
the words seem to
play in the right direction
as if I had
written the script all over you
now, you know I want to
imagine your dreams
becoming this reality
just say you
want to and
I will sculpt you
between every line
caressing arches
remapping . . .
your affections
like . . . I just discover you
wait . . . here's the kiss
in all the places

you thought I missed

tasting every part of you

here's the cure

my pen at the edge of intentions

loving every stroke

going in like more would never

be enough

see, a poem

never ends

this is temptation

whispering my come to

that fit

that taking me in

deep

like . . . like you want me 2

like I want 2 do

you again

thinking that once we begin

I would have to go all in

seeing, she's my love poem

and now

she knows it

A shared moment from

Love and The Conversation

Playing Temptation

She was that
first drink
She became my last
finding myself . . . drunk
in her emotions
consumed me
the taste of temptation
had me hungering
saying, "please"
it was like 'more' was all
I wanted to do
the pleasures of a kiss
whispering,
"take me"
let's make a love song
echoing
play me again
like a
fantasy
chasing the night away
thinking
she's got me gone

Complicated Passions After Midnight

Thoughts of temptation

my emotion

leaves my imagination

wandering

my wanting to love you deeper

call it: my

complicated passions

thinking the way

I do

knowing no one is going to love u

like I do

that last line,

I will hold

being who I am

surrendering my affections

I want u 2 love me 2

when u

are wanting like

it's

after midnight

I'll be the morning coming

thinking about u

N Side Of U

I've got a fever . . . that
burning n side of u
has me
hungering
heartbeats
from the echoes
find me drowning n your whispers when
you say my name
my wanting all of u
will have
no end
tasting the moments
this time around, these kisses
will become
the things you never want 2 miss
I've got u
I'm that surrender when
you're my
submission . . . that u come 2 when
u want me 2
take u . . . again
just whisper

Something About Me

She said she loved me, and yet
she married the other guy
she asked me "would we
still be friends?"
I told her
this was our end.
I wouldn't cross this line
have temptation calling me
2 give in
I needed 2 erase her memories
from my dreams
having them
would complicate me 2
"why,"
would never be my question
she was never
my answer
loving her as I loved myself
seems to have been
my weakness
living the life of an emotional creature
was still my status quo

Love Wanting an Answer

Love came
knocking
She was wanting,
wanted to know
asking
how she could be
the answer
to the moments beyond
my complications
knowing that my hunger for passion
was written all
over me
she didn't know
how much
only the traces she could see
she could only imagine
how deep
thinking she could take me
she
wanted my thoughts
I told her
She would have to surrender her dreams

The Tales of Dark Man Blues

I'm that night you long for
from your days of wondering
"Could he be?
Think of me as dreams, that
hunger calling out
saying, "I know u want 2"
no one like me
just wannabes in a world of misunderstanding
what love should be
having thoughts whispering, "please"
saying you love me
will bring temptation
the stories you write about
the dare 2 let
passion out
These are the moments I will
become u
writing on the pages
of a never-ending line
having my complicated passions echoing
the tales of
Dark Man Blues

The Other Side

The first time I saw u
I knew
we were meant 2 b
Gemini
U got me wanting
every side
of u
I'll be daring temptation
knowing it's
a product of my age
keeping me
away from you
the numbers
keep telling me
I want 2
be that fit, that "it"
u come 2
those innocence moments
of your affection
becoming my hunger when
u are wanting
like me

The Bridge

Nobody wanted me until

someone had me

I'm thinking, not misunderstanding

my role

here's the realness:

no playtime with my soul

my intentions

love without condition

no stop signs, looking for permission

no intervention

staying true to myself

loving this one like

no one else

not falling prey 2 the game when

I already have someone

whispering my name

never breaking

a heart

that could be mine

giving that positive time

building that

relationship bridge

Audience Participation

It was time to pay it forward
being about the truth
emboldened, they have become since
Trump spoke hope for them
I already knew
seeing that, the past is still the daily
things haven't changed; the more you think about it
you will see them the same
to see the big picture
you'll need to have input. that
would be
Audience Participation
something that didn't happen
in this election
no crying later when you had choice
the forty-three percent
made it clear
they have given us this end, and now
racism has stepped in
frontline bigotry
is now the spoken norm
this is your life

Last Chance

It's time to filibuster all the shit that's wrong
400 years gone
still the same
they plan these broken homes
playing it like a game
follow me, hear what I'm not saying
truth speaking
this is the hand being played
take away their names
give them shame
keep as many down as you can
have them help, too
give them some rules
watch them play it like fools
trying to keep up
we can keep them broken with this lie
tell them "This is your chance"
wasting your life away
on a false clue
check this past-time his-story
you'll see
he's still got you lost in his reality

No Loose Ends

End statement: me coming
from all ends
taking on foes, sometimes friends
dropping realness
being me
my pen on the verge of
how deep
I'll be saying
what I feel
no sugarcoating when
I do that
doing me, you see
no chasing
tomorrow
ain't promised
not for you, not even me
so, here's the deal
like George Clinton
"the bigger the headache the bigger the pill"
you feel
no loose ends
just drop n's

The Whisper of My Name

Poetry is my soul
the word flow takes me
got me thinking
the conversation over again
like the weather
ever-changing
taking chances on this romance
finding myself n 2 u
like the beginning and ending of that next line
when I can reach back inside
this book and make love
to your mind
one page at a time
just enough for u 2 give n
loving u like
insatiable
all the while, being
mischievous
knowing how much
I need u
to be
whispering my name

The Take Out

The Democrats didn't win
damn free college
gone until we get them back in
the GOP wasted 87 mil
trying to repeal
your medical bill
away
January Twenty First, the day
we gon' build that wall
I meant
fence
Border Patrol
not thinking about the fruits of labor
somebody got to pick
no doubt
hotel sleepaways
clean them
rooms
cooks, slaves
I mean
everyone has to undergo change
you will

Private Institutions

Nothing new

the same story under review

this is how America's

got you

prison pipeline

Black Gold

Incarcerated black souls

Institutions

did I say schools?

oh, I meant to

and yet

these are the crimes against you

that Jim Crow

all new

back to plantation you

his mission

1972

build them

fill them

replace them

damn...

let's try that again

The Best of Me

I am living Dark Man Blues
loving you
my condition, every moment
I am 2 be
thinking of you
the pleasure
I'm going through
living my dreams
painting you
imagine
the fixture our love
has come 2
those beautiful moments
I've got u
whispering
echoing
your affection
telling me
"I got u"
being my everyday love
come true
contemplating my Dark Man Blues

A New Name

We have survived your best
at our worst
still, you want more
as if slavery was not enough
these are moments
we can hold true
those things you never value
but you cling to
you remember segregation
voting rights
ghetto life
not just me, but poor whites
wanting to be me
all the while, trying to
extinguish the light
drug warfare
on the disenfranchised
not really true
you change the laws to suit you
call it what you want
even give it a new name
it's still racism

Endangered Species

Humankind defined as one with nature
the beginning
one, then two, plus me and now you
out of Africa, no class system
shades of beautiful
now you are no different
from me
yet, you try to be
rewriting the truth into lies
making up shit
as if I were blind
judgmental
you are not like me
you have become a virus
upon this flower
translation:
defiler of the land and the air we breathe
the creator of death
you are not humanity's last chance
but the ending of
Mankind's
Dark Man Blues

Imagining Freedom

My every day

one stop sign after another

proceeding with caution, giving thought

contemplating

trying not to be the news

I struggle

in this land of the free

finding myself, sometimes, in a daydream

not wanting this shit to be

my reality

it is said, "history will repeat itself"

think about

seeing that

Black Lives Matter

only to us

its time to make history

instead of waiting

to be

while imagining

freedom

Dark Man Blues

Other Titles

My N 2 U

Time Stamped

Beautiful Blindness

Painting America

The Written Confessions of DMB

Poem

Playing Temptation

Complicated Passions After Midnight

N Side Of U

Something About Me

Love Wanting an Answer

The Tales of Dark Man Blues

The Other Side

The Bridge

Audience Participation

Last Chance

No Loose Ends

The Whisper of My Name

The Take Out

Private Institutions

The Best of Me

A New Name

Cover Concept
Samuel Rain Benjamin

Cover Design
Eric DeVaughnn

Written by
Samuel Rain Benjamin

Dark Man Blues
The Series

Dark Man Blues/The Other Side

Dark Man Blues/John Bold

The Love of Dark Man Blues

www.ingramcontent.com/pod-product-compliance
Lightning Source LLC
Chambersburg PA
CBHW071946100426

42736CB00042B/2240